# Forew

C000261163

This book has been written to celebɪ
The Sheffield Cats Shelter which was estab

Although parts of our history are undocumented, this is our attempt to piece together the story of how we were founded and later became a lifeline for so many animals.

It has been fascinating to trawl through historical records, and to find that over the years, the Shelter has faced many of the problems that still challenge us today. Although the early years of our charity saw darker periods, our story is an important part of social history and an insight into our attitude towards animals. The history of The Sheffield Cats Shelter is therefore an important element in Sheffield's local history.

We rely on the generosity of donors and corporate supporters to carry on rescuing these cats, providing them with warmth, food, medical treatment, and above all love, until we can place them with a family or foster carer.

With your support, we can give every cat that comes into the Shelter the chance of a happy and healthy life in a loving home.

Ruby, who was nursed back to health after suffering cat flu.

༄ Acknowledgements ༄

Many people have contributed to the making of this book. Our thanks to past Committee Members and Trustees for their painstaking work in recording the history of our charity through Annual General Meeting (AGM) minutes and newsletters. Thanks also to Jody Virago for her research into the history of Jane Barker, which has helped us to write this book, and to Marina Lewycka for her help with editing. We also thank the Sheffield City Council and The Star Newspaper for allowing us to reproduce historic photographs which bring so much colour to our past.

Special thanks are due to all our staff, volunteers, and supporters, past and present. Without their dedication and challenging work, we wouldn't be able to run our charity, which helps so many animals in need of our support.

And lastly many thanks to you. By buying this book you will be helping us to put an end to the needless suffering of our feline friends, and providing a valuable resource for the animal lovers of Sheffield.

Fizz, *one of our much-loved elderly residents who had her very own room during her time at the Shelter.*

02

Contents

Appendices

Chapter 1 - Our History

"Pet euthanasia was the only option"

There are many reasons why a pet becomes homeless. Their owners may have passed away or be unable to look after them anymore, they may have been born stray, and in some heart-breaking cases they may have been abandoned. In the past, euthanasia for pets and domestic animals was widely practised and was often the only option. The Sheffield Cats Shelter was part of a movement originating in the C19th to seek a more humane solution to the problem of homeless animals.

Control to Care

Animal welfare has been an issue in the UK for over 200 years. One of the earliest enterprises that brought change to Sheffield was in 1873 when a local branch of the Society for the Prevention of Cruelty to Animals (SPCA), the forerunner to the RSPCA, was opened. Horses were the priority in those days because they were widely used for transportation and they were important to our industry. Welfare initiatives included the provision of horse troughs to give the animals a place to drink. The RSPCA chronicles one of the earliest troughs in Sheffield which was erected in Fitzalan Square in 1894, and remained there until the 1950s.

The original trough has been restored and can be seen at the RSPCA Animal Centre on Woodburn Road

Domestic animals, primarily cats and dogs, were not really thought about at that time, but in 1897 Jane Barker, who served on the Ladies Committee of the SPCA, set up a cat shelter. The earliest record in the Sheffield Archives lists "Miss Jane Barker's Home for Cats" at 27 Broomspring Lane.

Jane Barker was a philanthropist, with connections in high places. Within five years of founding the charity, she had secured the support of the Duchess of Portland and the Dowager Countess of Wharncliffe who had become patrons. The charity had by then also adopted the title "The Sheffield Shelter for Lost and Starving Cats".

The Duchess of Portland was a passionate animal lover. She kept stables for aging horses and ponies that were no longer useful as working animals, and dogs that needed homes. She was the first president of the Royal Society for the Protection of Birds and Vice President of the RSPCA. She was also elected as the third President of the Nottinghamshire Beekeepers' Association in 1907.

Winifred Anna Dallas-Yorke (The Duchess of Portland) by Philip de László (1912)

1897 was a prestigious year for Sheffield because Queen Victoria made her only visit to the city on 21 May. In celebration of her Diamond Jubilee, she attended the official opening of the new Town Hall. Amongst the guests that she received was the Duke of Portland. We do not know whether his wife, the Duchess, attended.

Although Jane Barker had the patronage of influential people, she clearly needed help from the working classes to run the charity and placed this advert in the local paper.

Sheffield Evening Telegraph - Monday 27 November 1905
SHEFFIELD CATS SHELTER – Wanted – respectable WOMAN, as Help to Caretaker; abstainer preferred; good character indispensable. – Apply evenings, 27 Collegiate cres

In the early 20th century, society's attitude towards animals was very different and at that time; animal control, rather than welfare was the primary concern. But a look at the history behind the domestication of cats in the UK helps to explain this.

The Long History behind the Domestication of Cats

Cats have lived alongside humans for millennia. It is commonly believed that the ancient Egyptians were first responsible for their domestication because they venerated cats, which is evidenced by the many Egyptian gods which are in their image. The increase in agriculture at that time would have attracted vermin which in turn would entice cats, and adds weight to this philosophy. Even today, feral cats will flock to and thrive in areas where they can find food, be it around a restaurant where there are edible scraps or on a farm with vermin to hunt. From around 8,000 BC it is thought that cats started to migrate from the Middle East to other parts of the world.

Studies have also found that leopard cats were starting to be domesticated independently in China around 5,500 BC. However, this line of partially domesticated cats leaves no trace in the domesticated populations of today.

Domestic cats were brought to Europe around 3000 years ago, by Greek and Phoenician traders. The Romans valued cats highly for pest control and the Roman Legions would have certainly taken cats with them as they moved through Gaul (modern day France) and eventually Britain.

However, cats started to get bad press with Europeans who destroyed them because they were associated with the Devil, witchcraft or evil. But cats were very useful in controlling the rodent population, and their mass destruction, because of unfounded fears, led to terrible consequences.

In the 14th century, the bubonic plague, often called the Black Death, spread across Europe. This deadly disease was transmitted to people by rat fleas. Almost one fourth of the entire population in Europe in the 1300's were killed by this plague. It was only then that people started to appreciate the value of cats and allowed them to multiply and attack the plentiful supply of rodents.

The association with witchcraft however, lasted for many years. Fairy tales always depict the wicked witch with her 'familiar' which is usually a black cat.

From being idolised by the Egyptians to being feared by the Europeans; and from being destroyed because of misjudged ideas to being allowed to propagate to kill rodents: history has shown that cats are among nature's great survivors.

Royal interest

But, a major change in the fortunes of the cat, certainly in the UK, started in the Victorian era. Although she was known for her love of dogs, the young Queen Victoria also owned two Blue Persian cats and in later years, she also bought a black and white Persian named White Heather which outlived her and was adopted by her son.

Victoria had a lonely childhood which is why historians believe that she found comfort in animals and became a devoted animal lover and promoter for animal rights. Particularly concerned about the treatment of domestic animals, she spoke out publicly against the practice of vivisection, and in 1840 became a patron of the Royal Society for the Prevention of Cruelty to Animals.

In the early C20th the Royal family influenced the whole country, and Victoria's appreciation of cats kick-started a new attitude towards their inimitable beauty and attraction. Popular images such as this started to appear:

A Victorian image of "Kittens Playing Piano"

The Royal family continued to publicly show their appreciation of cats. Victoria's granddaughter, Princess Victoria of Schleswig Holstein, and her daughter-in-law, Princess Alexandra of Wales, were well known for their love of cats and they both became actively involved in their welfare.

The first ever cat show was organized in 1871 at the Crystal Palace, but it was a lavish event, designed for the aristocracy and upper classes, who usually owned pedigree cats.

Attitudes towards cats were also changing because of the way that some Victorian authors portrayed them. Beatrix Potter and Lewis Carroll both wrote popular children's stories using anthropomorphism which promoted cats as friendly lovable animals.

These early 20th century influences made it fashionable amongst the upper classes to own a domestic cat, but the reality of the lives of working class people meant that their approach to animal welfare took longer to change. The cat population was out of control because neutering was not readily available. Animal control, rather than welfare was still a primary concern because cats were usually kept, not as pets, but to reduce the rodent population, and many lived on the streets in colonies.

The growing population of uncared for cats, along with their increasing popularity as pets, must have influenced Jane Barker to open the Cat Shelter. Like most animal charities, the Shelter had 'lethal chambers' where suffering and unwanted animals would be taken to die. By 1902 over 1,000 cats were being taken-in each year, but sadly, most of them were not re-homed as this entry from the Sheffield Red Book explains:

The Sheffield Red Book 1902: Page 53
SHELTER FOR LOST AND STARVING CATS, 27 BROOMSPRING LANE.

The Sheffield Shelter For Lost & Starving Cats was first opened in January 1897 and is doing increasingly useful work; the number of cats and kittens received during the present year amounting to 1,600. The object of the Shelter is not to provide a permanent home for cats, but to reduce the number of homeless creatures wandering about, unnoticed for, until they die of starvation or become victims of some form of cruelty. The majority of cats received have to be destroyed, owing to illness, accident and disease, and this is done in a merciful manner by means of chloroform. The Shelter is managed by a committee and supported solely by voluntary contributions. Patronesses, Her Grace the Duchess of Portland, and the Dowager Countess of Wharncliffe; hon. Secretary, Miss D Ibbotson; hon. Treasurer, Miss J. Barker, the Rookery, Broomhall park; hon, veterinary surgeon, Mr Tom C, Fletcher, M.R.C.V.S., 3 Ellin Street, Moor.

Through the first half of the 20th century, pet euthanasia was the only option for many people who, in war torn Britain, feared for their pets because of bombing, displacement and food rationing.

Gas and strong anaesthetics were used to put to sleep animals that were ill or homeless. This sounds horrific to us today, but it was more humane than other control measures that existed at the time, such as death by drowning or bludgeoning.

The summary on page 11 shows that within 23 years, the number of cats meeting this fate each year escalated to over 5,000.

Vinnie, *a timid kitten who was born to a feral mum but soon started to trust humans under the care of the Shelter staff.*

Amelie, *who came to the Shelter after being found living on the streets with her mum and siblings.*

Year	Number of Cats Admitted	Year	Number of Cats Admitted
1901	1,200	**1912**	Exceeding 3,700
1902	1,600	**1913**	Exceeding 4,000
1904	Exceeding 2,000	**1914**	Exceeding 4,000
1905	Exceeding 2,200	**1915**	No Numbers
1906	Exceeding 2,300	**1917**	Over 3,000
1907	Exceeding 2,500	**1918**	Over 3,000
1908	Exceeding 2,600	**1919**	3,800
1909	No Numbers	**1920**	3,000
1910	Exceeding 3,200	**1921**	3,600
1911	Exceeding 3,600	**1922**	4,700
		1923	5,580

It is however heartening to know that attempts were made to reunite lost cats with their owners. This is an example of the many adverts that appeared in the local press.

Sheffield Daily Telegraph. 10 October 1903
Found, Tabby Persian cat – taken to Cats Shelter, Broomspring La

By 1913, stray dogs were also taken in but sadly to the same fate

The Sheffield Red Book 1913: Page 237.
SHELTER FOR LOST AND STARVING CATS, 106, GELL STREET
(Entrance Broomspring Lane)

Is doing increasingly useful work, the number of cats and kittens received during the past year exceeding 4,000. The object of the shelter is not to provide a permanent home for cats, for to reduce the number of homeless creatures wandering about, unnoticed, uncared for, until they die of starvation or become victims of some form of cruelty. The majority of cats received have to be destroyed, owing to illness, accident and disease, and this is done in a merciful manner by means of chloroform. There is also accommodation for a limited number of cats and small dogs as "boarders" at a moderate charge per week. Lethal chambers for the merciful destruction of dogs are now kept on the premises. The Shelter is managed by a committee and supported solely by voluntary contributions. Hon secretary, Mrs. Millward, 67 Wolstenholme road; hon. Treasurer. Miss J Barker, the Rookery, Broomhall park; hon. veterinary surgeon, Mr. Jos, Abson, 53 Norfolk-street.

The British Veterinary profession began in 1785 when the Odiham Agricultural Society was founded to promote agriculture and industry, specifically by caring for horses, using the science that was available. This led to the establishment of the London Veterinary College in 1791, which was the start of the development of veterinary science and a professional group dedicated to animal medicine. Initially, the veterinary profession was centred around the horse, and this remained the focus for many years because of the needs of both industry and the Army. Over time, the interest of the profession spread to cattle and other livestock, then to dogs and eventually other companion animals.

Although veterinary legislation has been in force since 1881, it was not until 1956 that the British Small Animal Veterinary Association was set up, which now promotes the welfare of pets.

It may seem shocking to us that, along with other charities, the Shelter put so many animals to sleep because they were unwell. But these were different times and we cannot judge their actions by today's standards. Veterinary treatment, at best, would have been basic and expensive. Charities simply didn't have the resources or specialist help to save animals that needed treatment.

The Shelter was clearly affected by WWI (1914-1918) when Jane Barker placed this notice in the local press:

Sheffield Daily Telegraph: Tuesday 25th August 1914

Cats and Dogs

The hon, secretary of the Cats Shelter writes:

It has been brought to our notice that, owing to the probability of unusual distress in this city, numbers of poor people may feel compelled to part with their cat or dog. Whilst we hope that this may not be the case, we desire to inform the public that, should anyone be in this sad position – unable to spare even a few coppers – their cat or dog may be taken to the Sheffield Cats Shelter 106, Gell Street. And humanely destroyed there free of charge.

Despite the wording in this notice, Jane Barker and her companions were clearly compassionate people who loved cats as much as we love them today. This extract from a letter sent in 1989 to the Shelter from Kathleen Spikesley, who wanted to share her memories, shows how dedicated she was to the charity.

I was introduced to two charming spinsters who lived in a large Victorian house in Collegiate Crescent, namely the Misses Barker, ladies of some means who were devoted to cats and had several of their own. They told me that they had commenced the Cats Shelter in Gell Street, and employed a man called Mr Westran (also a devoted cat lover) who also drove the van for the shelter. These two dear ladies had a grand conservatory in their grounds with a portion reserved for cat rescue. When people like myself found a stray, and did not wish to walk as far as Gell Street, the Misses Barker would take the cat from them at their home.

If a cat was injured or had the mange, then they would put it to sleep in one of two gas chambers that they had, in order to put an end to the cats suffering. If a stray was in good condition, then it was fed and looked after until Mr Westran came, collected the animal and took it to the main Shelter on Gell Street.

Although pet ownership may have flourished briefly during the years between the two world wars, World War II saw a terrible mass destruction of pets, which was fuelled by the government, who viewed pet ownership as a drain on valuable resources. When war was declared, the Home Office issued a pamphlet saying that dogs would not be allowed into air raid shelters, and this was reported by the BBC. During the following few days, thousands of people either abandoned their pets or took them to animal shelters, to be destroyed.

This mass destruction eased after a few days, but many people were shocked by what had happened. However, life remained very difficult for pet owners during the war. There are many documented stories of people being fined for wasting food on pets. Dogs were the main target, but cat ownership also came under fire. A Home Office anti-cat briefing was leaked to journalists which stated that 'Too many of this country's 7 million cats are overfed, given portions of meat and fish which, to a man, would be the equivalent of a 3lb joint every lunchtime.' It was also widely reported that cats consumed 40 million gallons of milk a year and the Chancellor considered a cat tax.

Many people simply abandoned their cats to the streets, which just fuelled the growth of cat colonies, that remained a problem in the post war years.

Sheffield Daily Telegraph: Monday 23 October 1939
CATS BEWILDERED BY BLACKOUT, MANY KILLED AND HURT

The blackout has caused a record number of accidents to cats. R.S.P.C.A. officials are urging the public to care better care of them. Dozens of cats have been found mutilated. The Sheffield Cats Shelter is being kept very busy dealing with injured pets, most of which have to be destroyed.

"I am advising people to keep their cats in after six o'clock at night", said Mrs, J. Barton, in charge of the Cats Shelter.

"It is a mistaken idea that cats can see in dark. They are afraid of darkness and many are getting hurt or killed.

"The accidents during the last two weeks have been grievous.

"I have never seen such pitiful sights and there will be many injured pets that are not found by anyone".

It is heart-breaking to think what these cats suffered, but the least of their problems would have been seeing in the dark. We now know that cats have superior eyesight.

We can assume that pet ownership became popular after WWII, but euthanasia was used as late as the 1960s. When the Shelter moved to Travis Place in 1964, the sign by the door still carried the words 'cats humanely destroyed'. But attitudes were shifting and by the 1970s, the Sheffield Cats Shelter had changed its focus to caring for cats that needed help and had by now become a refuge for homeless felines.

The Sheffield Lord Mayor, Winifred Mary Golding, shows her support for the Shelter in 1978.

Today, our charity gives every cat that we care for, shelter, food and warmth, as well as any medical treatment that it might need. And every cat is neutered, vaccinated and microchipped before being re-homed. We have come a long way since 1897 and we are sure that if Jane Barker could see what we do today, she would be very proud of our work.

An entry from our Newsletter in Spring 1990 tells the story of a cat, Whiskey, that was brought to the Shelter when it's owner was taken ill. The owner unfortunately died, while the cat was in our care, but he had left instructions that it should be put sleep on the event of his death. The Shelter fought this and won the right for the cat to stay in their care. Whiskey was eventually found a new home.

Jasper, *a friendly boy who came to the Shelter with 5 other cats after being abandoned by their owner.*

15

Chapter 2 -
The Life of Jane Barker

"Jane was a philanthropist and an animal lover"

Family History

Jane Barker was born into a wealthy and relatively large family. The daughter of Henry and Sarah, she entered the world on 1 November 1866 and was baptised on Christmas Day that year.

The annual census of 1851 places Samuel Barker (her grandfather) living with his wife and seven children in Mexborough. Their eldest child, Henry Barker, followed in his father's footsteps and became an 'earthenware manufacturer'. When Samuel died in 1865, at the age of 56, Henry and his brother Samuel Jnr took over the Don Pottery, which had been acquired by the Barker family in the 1830s.

Henry Barker married Sarah Hall in the mid 1860's. By 1871 they had five children and the census of that year shows that they were living in Mexborough along with John (7), Mary Beatrice (5), Jane (4), Henry Shelly (2), and Earnest (10 months). The family clearly had wealth as their household also included a governess, a nurse for the baby and toddler, a cook and two housemaids.

Like his father, Henry died at a very early age. He was 48.

The Sheffield Independent. 10 March 1876

DEATH OF HENRY BARKER ESQ., of MEXBRO'. - We have to record the death of H. Barker Esq., who expired yesterday morning at a quarter past ten o'clock at his residence in Mexbro'. Deceased, who has been ailing for some time, was in his 48th year. Mr Barker was one of the principals in connection with the Don Iron Works, Mexbro', and the Don Potteries, Swinton. He was highly respected, and will be interred at Mexbro' Church, on Monday next.

By 1881, the Barker family had moved to 27 Collegiate Crescent, Sheffield. Five years after Henry's death, the census describes his widow Sarah, as head of household and living 'on her own means'. The children Mary Beatrice (15), Jane (14), Henry Shelley (12), and Earnest (10) are all described as "scholar". Presumably John at the age of 17, had moved out of the family home. At that time, the family employed a live-in governess and teacher, a cook and two housemaids.

The 1891 census tells us that Sarah had not remarried and remained head of household. The entries for both Mary Beatrice, aged 25 and Jane, aged 24 state that they have 'no occupation' but by this time, Jane had set up the Cats Shelter. Henry Shelley is described as an "articled law clerk" and Ernest is a medical student. The household also lists two medical servants (Lizzie Rollinson and Clara Babbington) as well as a domestic servant and two housemaids. Shortly after the census, Sarah died on 13 April 1891 aged 56.

The 1901 census records Mary Beatrice, aged 35 as head of the household, living with Jane, aged 34. Both sisters are described as 'living on own means'. They have three other residents in the household: their cook, Elizabeth Holmes (29), and two housemaids, Hilda Dronfield (22) and Lizzie Copely (19).

In 1911, Mary Beatrice, aged 45, remains the unmarried head of the household. She lives with Jane, aged 44, also unmarried, and three domestic staff, Hannah Hudson (31), Emma Hudson (27) and Liggie Kitson (18). On the night of the 1911 census they also have a visitor staying with them, a Charlotte Webb who is aged 70.

The wills from the Barker family indicate their wealth:

The Don Pottery 1801-1893

When Henry died in 1876 he left £50,000 entirely to his wife Sarah who, when she died in 1891 at the Rookery, Broomhall Park, Sheffield she left £80,390.

The pottery closed in 1893, two years after the death of Sarah.

In 1876, £50,000 was a substantial amount and £80,000 is equivalent to approx. £2 million in today's money. This inheritance meant that Mary Beatrice and Jane were financially independent and had no need to marry for financial security.

Today, 27 Collegiate Crescent is called Hopton House. It's an imposing Grade II listed building which has been extended and divided into luxury flats and office space.

Mary Beatrice died on 27 October 1951 aged 85. An obituary from her sister Jane reads:

Sheffield Telegraph: 28 October 1951

Barker – On Oct 27 at the Rookery, 27 Collegiate Crescent at Sheffield. Mary Beatrice, a dearly beloved sister. Service at the Crematorium, City Road. No flowers by request. In Heavenly love abiding.

The Cripples Aid Association later printed their own eulogy (see page 20).

The Sheffield Cripples Aid Association - End Year report for 1951

"In presenting the fifty-first annual report for committee record, with deep regret the death of Miss Barker. Miss Barker spent a lifetime in furthering the interests of all cripples in Sheffield and until a few days before she was called to Higher Service, she maintained her keen interest in the work of the Association.

She was greatly loved and her passing was a personal loss to all."

Five years after the death of her sister, Jane Barker died on Christmas Eve, 1956. She was still living at Collegiate Crescent which had been her home for over seventy-five years. We do not know when or if she ever stopped being involved with the work of the Shelter, but we know that she dedicated her life to caring for cats.

Sheffield Telegraph. 27 December 1956

Barker – On Dec 24 1956 at, 27 Collegiate Crescent. Jane in her 91st year, daughter of the late Henry Barker of Mexborough and very dear sister-in-law of Mrs Shelley Barker, Service at City Road Crematorium, tomorrow. Friday, at 3.45 pm. No flowers by request.

Georgie, *who was abandoned by his owners when they moved.*

Jane Barker and
The Sheffield Cripples
Aid Association

"It later became known as the Sunbeam Club"

As well as her love of animals, Jane Barker was a humanitarian who, along with her sister Mary Beatrice, established a charity for disabled children. The Sheffield Cripples Aid Association was set up in 1900 and although it had no relationship with the Cat Shelter, it is worthy of note because of its importance to Jane. The charity later became known as the Sunbeam Club for Crippled Children, and while the terms used in the listing below are now outdated, the Association clearly tried to help disadvantaged children.

The Sheffield Red Book 1920: Page 234

Sheffield Cripples' Aid Association (Sunbeam Club): - This Association was formed in 1900 by the Misses Barker, its object being to brighten the lives of crippled children and to enable them later, if possible, to earn their own living.

This 1942 entry in Kelly's directory provides more detail:

1942 Kelly's Directory: Page lxxxv

Sheffield Cripples' aid Association (Sunbeam Club) - This Association was formed in 1900 by the Misses Barker, its object being to brighten the lives of crippled children and to enable them later, if possible, to earn their own living. The membership is now over 1.700. The homes of children are visited every month and efforts are made to provide the help which is necessary. Spinal and other invalid carriages are lent, and assistance is given towards obtaining surgical appliances and crutches when required. The Association maintains Loxley House Convalescent Home, for crippled children who require special care and the benefits of fresh air. Patients are admitted for four weeks or longer at the discretion of the committee. The home is supported by voluntary contributions. A cot may be endowed in perpetuity for £1,000, or maintained by a payment of £50 per year. The office of the Association is 23 Claremont Crescent 10, President, the Lord Mayor; chairman, Lt.-Col. H.S.Walker; hon. Treasurer, Miss B.A.W. Taylor, 5 Endcliffe Crescent 10; secretary, Miss A. Harrison.

The convalescent home referred to above is Loxley House at Hillsborough. It was later used by the Sheffield Sea Cadet Corps, as a base for many years. In 1996, the house was put up for sale and was bought by the property developers Campbell Homes who turned it into luxury flats and apartments.

By 1931, the charity had attracted influential patrons including The Duke & Duchess of Norfolk, and The Earl and Countess Wharncliffe. The Lord Mayor and Master Cutler of Sheffield were Presidents and the Lord Bishop was vice President.

These dignitaries clearly helped the charity's success as demonstrated in this extract from The Sheffield Daily Independent:

Sheffield Independent: 28 January 1931
Sheffield Women As We Know Them
The Misses M and J Barker, From 26 to 1,700

One naturally associates the names of those two well-known Sheffield philanthropists, Miss Mary Barker and Miss Jane Barker, with the Sheffield Cripples Aid Association.

It is a natural also that should be pictured, as I saw them this week, presiding happily, yet busily over the tea urns at the crippled children's tea parties at the Cutler's Hall.

The Misses Barker can look back gratefully over their years from the day when they first discovered a means of grouping the cripples together in an organisation, to today, when there are over 1,700 members in the association.

In co—operation with Miss B.A.W. Taylor, the present treasurer, Miss Olive Hargreaves, Miss E Wigfall. Mrs Alice Laycock, and several other stalwarts of the cause, who still have the interests of the cripples at heart. They started the "Sunbeam Club" or what was known among the young crippled members as the "Sunbeam School".

Meetings were held once a fortnight in the old Ebenezer Schools and later at the Friends Meeting House, Hartshead.

Many of the cripples, Miss Mary Barker told me in a chat I had with her, could neither read nor write and many of them had no interest in life whatsoever.

Those were in the days before Dr Ralph Williams, the then School Medical Officer of Health, with his love of crippled children, brought the needs of a day school for crippled children profitably before the public and before the King Edward VII Hospital at Rivelin stated its work of curing.

Miss Barker told me that the membership at the inception of the small club in May 1900 was 26. The only means they had of recruiting members was by approaching crippled people they met in the streets and asking them to join.

Today with their large membership and splendid organisation, they are faced with the problem of finding suitable employment for the trained young people., she told me, one young man was earning his living as a sign-writer. Pointing to the motto of the Association, used in the decoration of the room "By Love Serve One Another", she told me with pride that it was the work of a young member who had only one hand.

The economic effects following World War II and the introduction of the National Health Act in 1948 (the welfare state), meant it was no longer viable to maintain the Children's home at Loxley. It moved to smaller premises at Dore, but the need for the charity declined and it closed in the 1950s.

The Sheffield Cats Shelter remains grateful to Jane Barker for her generosity and work in those early days. Although the Shelter today is unrecognisable from when the charity was first set up, Jane Barker's 'Home for lost cats' provided a valuable service to the public and evolved into the caring organisation that we are today.

Figaro, *who lived at the Shelter for nine months before he found his forever home.*

Chapter 3 -
Management of the Shelter

"1984 was a turning point in the management of the Shelter"

"Every generation imagines itself to be more intelligent than the one that went before it, and wiser than the one that comes after it."
- George Orwell

The Sheffield Cats Shelter has always been managed by a Committee, which initially comprised a secretary, a treasurer and a vet. This format, recorded in the Sheffield Red Book, remained the same until the 1930s, but the Committee grew in numbers listing eleven Members in 1941 along with our patron, Her Grace the Duchess of Portland.

Attempts to regulate charities in the UK had been ineffective until the mid C19th when the Charities Commission was established in 1853. Previous attempts at reforming charities had been opposed by various interest groups including the church, the courts, businesses and universities. It wasn't until the Charities Act 1960, that a national register of Charities was introduced which gave the Commission investigative powers. This presumably prompted the Management Committee to register the Shelter with the Commission on 8 October 1963 under the name of 'The Gell Street Cats Shelter' which was changed in 1970 to 'The Sheffield Cats Shelter'.

Records of our work in the 1970s are incomplete, but the 1983 AGM minutes tell the story of a dispute which led to a turning point in the Shelter's management policies.

In 1983, the eight members of Management Committee decided that the interests of the charity would be best served by forming a trust to control the assets of the Shelter, which totalled £26,307. To this end, they approached the Charity Commission for permission to sell Travis Place, to raise funds for a purpose-built cattery.

Objections were raised by a 'pressure group', led by a former Secretary and Treasurer, who filed a complaint to the Charity Commission and accused the Management Committee of mismanagement and trying to close the Shelter against the wishes of the public. This attracted a fair amount of publicity and the story appeared in the Sheffield Telegraph.

Eventually, a meeting was held on 24 April 1983 between the Management Committee, their solicitor and the Charity Commission. The outcome of the meeting was an agreement that the Committee had in fact acted responsibly, but that steps must be taken to safeguard the future finances of the charity.

The 1983 AGM minutes reflect that "for the last 25 years, the charity had relied heavily on 'older people' and that survival was now in the hands of the younger, new 1984 Committee". We can conclude that it was at this point that the Committee Members became Trustees of the charity, which was a major turning point.

1983. A volunteer with two residents of the Shelter.

Although the sale of Travis Place didn't happen, from 1984, the Trustees did start to make decisions that modernised the charity, including the introduction of a neutering policy, alterations to Travis Place, new and innovative fundraising ideas, and the employment of staff. A new constitution was filed with the Charity Commission in 1994 which remained the basis of our structure until 2016 when we incorporated.

As well as holding regular meetings to discuss finance and other issues affecting the charity, the Trustees have also held AGMs since 1912, to keep members updated. The public were invited to the first AGM at the Cutler's Hall.

Sheffield Daily Telegraph: Saturday 11 May 1912
SHEFFIELD SHELTER FOR LOST AND STARVING CATS
106, Gell Street

THE FIRST PUBLIC ANNUAL Meeting of the above institution will be held in the CUTLERS HALL, on MONDAY AFTERNOON, MAY 13th, at 3.30.

Speaker, Mr Arthur Coke, of London, Secretary of Our Dumb Friends League.

All those who are interested in the welfare of animals are requested to attend.

In later years, AGMs were often held at the Friends Meeting House, but since 2000, we have moved to the more relaxed surroundings of the Fat Cat Pub, on Alma Street, to hold this annual event.

The policies and finances of the charity have always been managed by the Committee / Trustees, but the day-to-day running of the Shelter was the responsibility of a resident caretaker or warden until 2001. Countless people have taken on this role which has proved to be a popular job. When the vacancy came up in 1988, there were over 80 applicants for the post! Perhaps this is confirmation of the magnetism of cats.

Jane Barker hired live-in caretakers to run the Shelter, and advertised for cleaning women to help with the chores. Sometimes she took on a married couple who could fill both the warden and cleaner roles.

In 1986, our warden Ian married Marie. And as a show of dedication, Marie spent her honeymoon hand rearing a 10-day old kitten which had been dumped in a bin.

The caretaker role eventually morphed to resident warden, and those living at Travis Place had a small attic bedroom (which is now our office), plus a lounge, kitchen and bathroom on the first floor, which have now all been converted to 'cat' rooms. As they were on-site, the wardens undertook a wide range of duties including cleaning, feeding, taking cats to the vets and handling adoptions. This was a heavy workload, but volunteers came in daily to help.

1983: The Shelter relies on volunteer help.

Wardens were expected to cope with a host of problems including the unexpected, such as rounding up cats that had been let out to roam the streets during a break-in in 1987.

Until the 1980s the Shelter opened to the public daily between 9.00am and 10.00pm to take in cats and receive visitors looking for lost pets, or wanting to adopt. These gruelling hours were reduced in 1988 to help the warden and by 1990, seven-day staffing was in place when the first two employees were taken on. A further reduction in visiting hours from 1.30pm to 5.00pm was implemented in 1995, and the Shelter started to close to visitors on Tuesdays and Thursdays.

The last resident warden resigned in 2001. Following her departure, a 6-month review was held to evaluate the efficacy of employing a full-time warden, which concluded that the charity would be better served by a non-resident warden. By this time, we were making better use of the local veterinary practice, leaving cats that needed overnight care with them which negated the need to have someone on hand 24/7 at the Shelter.

Over the years, we have reviewed the necessity and efficacy of opening times, taking account of staffing levels, the availability of volunteers, and in recent years, the impact of technology and social media. Although our opening hours are now limited, we are happy for people to visit by appointment.

Management of the Shelter has changed dramatically in recent years, particularly because of technology, which has brought many challenges, as well as advantages to the way that we work.

We first embraced technology in the 21st century and sent our first e-mail in 2000. We also began to process gift-aid that year. Our website domain was established in 2002, and the website itself was updated and redesigned in 2006, 2015 and in 2017 to reflect our new image. Technology has boosted our fundraising efforts including the use of eBay to sell donated items and social media to promote fundraising activities as well as connecting with our members.

Incorporation

The current Trustees of the charity inherited an organisation that was rapidly becoming out-dated and in need of modernisation to survive in a competitive world. A financial and PR review led to a major decision to incorporate the charity and The Sheffield Cats Shelter was registered as a limited company in 2016, although we didn't start trading as such until 2017. This is an important part of our ongoing modernisation which we hope will help to secure the charity for many years.

The Trustees, who are now Directors of the Shelter have a continuing responsibility to ensure the future of the charity, but remain reliant on the support of staff, volunteers and the public.

Chapter 4 -
Our buildings and locations

"Animal charities pulled together during the war"

The Sheffield Cats Shelter first opened at 27 Broomspring Lane as 'Miss Jane Barker's Home for Lost Cats' and remained there until 1905 when it moved to 106 Gell Street. In 1931, it relocated to 112-114 Gell Street. The buildings that we occupied have now all been demolished to make way for redevelopment and private homes have been built on each site.

Broomspring Lane at the corner of Gell Street in or around 1905. This corner is now an open space with a children's play area.

Visitors could bring cats and dogs to the door, but the Shelter was also proactive and collected stray animals found roaming the streets. A van was procured to transport the animals.

This photo was taken in 1929. The driver is William Shaw who died in 1931.

His obituary in the local press was very short:

Sheffield Independent: Wednesday 1 April 1931

SHAW, - On March 28th, at 112 Gell street, William Shaw, for twelve years, valued caretaker at the Sheffield Cats Shelter. Deeply regretted.

One of our supporters, Julie Major, tells us that in 1960, as an eight-year-old, she lived in Monmouth Street with her parents and grandparents. They had a tortoiseshell cat called Trixie which they got from Tom who ran the Shelter on Gell Street. She used to take old newspapers to Tom, and one day when she knocked on his door, a voice said "come in" but when she tried the handle the door was locked. She found out later that Tom had a talking parrot, who had responded to her knock!

The 1920s saw a boom in the economy which included a sharp increase in the use of telephones, as new styles of phones were introduced and rental costs became more accessible. A new Central Automatic Exchange was set up in Sheffield in the 1920s and the Shelter must have been one of the earliest subscribers. The 1924 edition of Kelly's Directory lists the Shelter along with our telephone number, Central 656.

Sheffield Independent: 8 December 1923
SHEFFIELD CATS SHELTER

106. Gell Street (Entrance Broomspring Lane). The public are asked to help in clearing the City of lost, diseased and suffering cats. Lost cats fetched FREE OF CHARGE. Ring up Central 656

From records that are available, we believe that we amalgamated with the RSPCA in the unstable years before World War II and this association lasted for several years. Animal charities in Sheffield worked together during and after WWII. Minutes from the RSPCA 76th Annual Report, in 1949, include an account from the Horses Rest Home as well as this extract about the Cat Shelter:

76th Annual Report (1949)

CATS SHELTERS. 112/114 Gell St. During the year this shelter dealt with an increased number of cats and dogs, the numbers being 5942 cats and 202 dogs. The total for stray cats was 260 compared with 1977. Other animals dealt with totalled 4.

218 ATTERCLIFFE COMMON. At the beginning of the year, Mrs Hollis resigned on the grounds of ill-health after 9 years service, and Mrs M. Hibberd was appointed and we are pleased to report that her services have been very satisfactory. At this shelter 2045 cats and 755 dogs were humanely destroyed being a slight increase in cats but a reduction in the number of dogs. In addition, 5 other animals were dealt with. The number of stray cats received, 300 was in increase of 40 Over 1948. At these two shelters 2447 animals were destroyed free.

The Sheffield Archives confirm that we ran a second branch at 331 Attercliffe Common from 1936 as this entry in Kelly's Directory illustrates:

1940
Kelly's Directory: page lxxxiv

Cats' Shelter, 112 & 114 Gell Street. First opened in 1897. The branch at 331 Attercliffe Common was opened in 1936. Open daily, up to 10 pm. The shelter is a temporary refuge, where cats are provided with food and warmth until claimed, sold or destroyed. Provision is also made for boarding cats; dogs as well as cats are humanely destroyed. Miss Edith Atkins, 28 Mylnhurst road, Ecclesall, hon secretary; Miss J Barker, 27 Collegiate crescent, hon, treasurer.

The Attercliffe Branch eventually merged with the RSPCA and the Gell Street Shelter remained independent as the Sheffield Cats Shelter. On her death in 1956, Jane Barker left the proceeds of 112-114 Gell Street, in trust to Mrs G Thorpe and Mrs D G Packham. They sold it and purchased 1 Travis Place on 1 May 1964.

1 Travis Place, in 1964. The sign reads:

The Sheffield Cats Shelter

Tel 24441

Cats Humanely Destroyed

Boarders Received

Mrs Packham died on 13 October 1969 and Mrs Thorpe appointed Mrs H Maw to be the new joint owner. Mrs Maw and Mrs Thorpe became life Trustees of the building in Travis Place.

An entry in The Sheffield and Telegraph Year Book 1965/66 records our move to Travis Place.

The Sheffield and Telegraph Year Book
1965/66. Page 129

Cats' Shelter, 1 Travis Place (off Clarke Street) 10
Late Gell Street. Open daily 9am to 10pm. (Tel 24441)
hon. Secretary, Miss J Julien, 1 Collegiate Crescent, 10. hon. Treasurer A Thorpe, 785 Chesterfield Road, 8.

Our building in 1976.

The sign reads:

Sheffield Cats Shelter

(A Voluntary Charity)

Always open for stray cats in need. Open for boarders 1April to 30 Sept. Hours 10am to 1pm 2pm to 6pm Tel 24441, Warden (blank), Secretary H A Maw

Our building in 2017.

From the outside, there are very few differences from how it looked in 1976. But inside, things have changed dramatically.

The first significant improvements to the building happened in 1984, when a £5,800 legacy from a former Committee Member funded several improvements, including new and hygienic flooring, rewiring, new heaters and Expel air fans, and a kitchen renovation, including the installation of a new sink and units.

Male and female cats had historically been kept in separate rooms because neutering was too expensive to contemplate. But a large donation in 1985 was used to finance a one-year trial to neuter all cats. This was so successful that it became a permanent policy the following year and remains in place today.

We do however take in many pregnant cats and mums with litters, and in recognition of the exceptional care that they need, a maternity room was installed in 1986 which was modernised ten years later:

We now have a modern maternity unit with facilities to help mums and their litters.

Our maternity unit

Harrier, an orphan kitten, being hand fed whist in maternity.

1986 also saw the installation of a burglar and smoke alarms, and the construction of a reception desk along with the purchase of a new filing cabinet. We also acquired a commercial tin opener!

In 1988, a jumble room was created in the cellar to hold donated items that we could sell at our 'Yard Sales'. We also built our first infirmary by claiming space from the 'females room', which housed pregnant cats and mums with litters. To help create more space we ran a concurrent appeal for Foster Carers to take in pregnant queens.

Substantial building work was carried out in 1992. including a new roof, refurbishment of the warden's flat and the installation of a security mesh in the yard. We also installed an Economy 7 metre to reduce heating costs.

Our policy is to reduce energy costs, and we also aim to be environmentally friendly. We therefore installed solar panels in 2011 and with the generous help of 'Support Adoption for Pets', we were able to put in a more efficient heating system to compliment them.

But by far the biggest refurbishment undertaken was in 1996 when £34,250 was spent on improvements, along with another £58,527 the following year. This is a huge amount but our building needed remedial structural work, including the rebuilding of the yard.

Refurbishment in 1996.

The floor plans were reproduced in a newsletter;

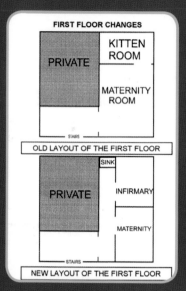

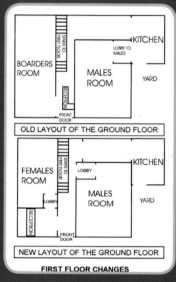

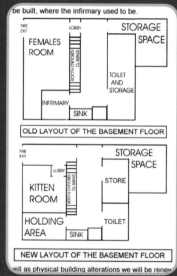

21st OCTOBER 1996

THE OLD KITTEN AND MATERNITY ROOM

The builders had moved onto the second phase of the refurbishment when the new cages arrived. The cages were in two configurations there were several 4 ft cages and several 6 ft cages.

The 4 ft cages were the first to arrive and they were installed into the new infirmary room. However the 6 ft cages proved impossible to get through the doors of the new rooms so they were sent back and a solution was discussed on how to get the 6ft cages into the maternity room.

28th OCTOBER 1996

THE NEW RECEPTION

The final stage of this part of the refurbishment involved tidying up the new reception and installing the new heaters.

5th DECEMBER 1996

REBUILDING THE YARD

Although the builders had started preliminary work on the basement area, a solution to the problem of reconstructing the yard was found and work started immediately on re-building the area.

19th MAY 1997

INSTALLING THE NEW CAGES

It was quite a struggle but Joe and Corky (the builders) along with the people from Shoreline (supplied the cages) were able to get all the cages up to the maternity room.

19th MAY 1997

INSTALLING THE NEW CAGES

Once the cages were up in their respective rooms, it was simply a matter of assembling which was done by a work man from Shoreline.

24th MARCH 1997

THE NEW HOLDING AREA AND KITTEN ROOM

New shelves were set up in the new kitten room to allow the kittens to sleep up off the floor if they wish too.

12th MAY 1997

REBUILDING THE KITCHEN

With all the kitchen equipment plumbed back in and all the plastering and tiling finished, it was time for the painters to paint the walls a lovely shade of white.

27th JANUARY 1997

REBUILDING THE YARD

Once the builders had finished the outside walls, they went to work on rebuilding the support pillars that will eventually take up the weight of the concrete yard.

Many thanks must also be given to the companies and individuals who donated money towards our cages appeal.

Bass Breweries
Sissons
Paul Bellamy
J. Hague and Jimbo the cat
Max & Rosemary Telfer
Miss K. Osborn

The Sheffield Junior Chamber of Commerce offered to manage a project to refurbish our yard in 1998. This was done the following year, with the help of donations from local businesses.

We have continued to improve and update our building and in:

- 2004, new windows were fitted to several rooms and the old warden's lounge was converted to a cat room.

- 2009, structural work was completed to enable the building to withstand the elements

Internal refurbishments and improvements to Cat rooms are an ongoing project and have included numerous upgrades including:

Room 2

2011. During refurbishment

2014. A separate pen was built for cats that needed space to be alone.

Room 5

The old domestic kitchen that was once part of the warden's accommodation was updated and made into communal cat room 5, in 2013/14. Much of the work was done by our volunteer handyman Robert, so we dedicated the room to his cat Temp, who had recently passed away. Temp acquired this name because Robert had adopted him as a kitten on a 'temporary' basis. Twenty years later, he was still living with him.

Temp taking a nap after helping with the building work.

Room 5, refurbished in loving memory of Temp the cat.

Our reception area has also seen many changes. It's very cramped but our staff and volunteers persevere.

A volunteer helps with admin work in our reception.

Despite the disadvantages of adapting a residential property, the layout of our building does have some benefits. Most cats that are ready to adopt are socialised with other cats by sharing a room. This is preferable to keeping them in individual cages and it also allows the cats to acclimatise to human contact which is great preparation for rehoming.

Our building has gone through many refurbishments, but we are chronically short of space. We have long-held aspirations to move to a building that better suits our needs. In 1984, the desire to sell Travis Place and acquire a purpose-built cattery led to change in the way that the Shelter was managed. In 1987, a fundraising drive was proposed to pay for a new building, and this theme was raised again in 1992, when our Chairperson expressed a hope that we could start the next century in new premises. We still have this dream.

Truffle, *who was found living as stray.*

43

Chapter 5 - Our work today

"Every penny helps"

Thankfully, society today has as a better understanding of the value that pets can bring to our lives, and we have more respect for the animals that share our world. Despite the very different aims of our charity from when it was founded, The Sheffield Cats Shelter has built on the work of Jane Barker, and is now a modern and forward looking organisation.

Our Values and Aims - Our Articles of Association state that:

'The Objects are for the public benefit the relief and prevention of suffering and distress amongst cats in need of care and attention and the advancement of the welfare of cats by any such means as are charitable, according to the laws of England and Wales'

What this means is that we:

• never put a healthy cat to sleep

• ensure all cats in our care receive any medical treatment that they need

• will do our best to rehome every cat that we care for.

> A 2016 survey by the Pet Food Manufacturing Association estimates that 17% of households in the UK are cat owners and the cat population is around 7.5 million.

Our mission is to find loving homes for homeless or neglected cats, and we do this by:

• rescuing cats that need shelter because they have lost their carer or home;

• prioritising cats who are most at risk because they have lost their human or are roaming the streets;

• arranging treatment for physical and behavioural problems, regardless of cost;

• providing exceptional care for every cat; and giving them a "home from home" environment;

• finding the right family for each cat so that their needs and personality are catered for;

• providing ongoing advice and support to cat owners;

• educating and advising on all aspects of cat care;

• never giving up on any cat.

Rupert, *who came to the Shelter suffering from chronic cat flu but was adopted to lovely home.*

Our Foster Programme

Most cats that we care for find loving homes, but unfortunately, some are overlooked for adoption because of potentially high veterinary fees. Typically, these are older cats or those with chronic medical problems and we have found that the best way to help these animals is to place them under our Long-Term Foster Programme. This means that they get to live with a family for the rest of their lives, but remain under our care because the Shelter meets additional medical or food costs that are over and above the routine care that all cats need. The costs are high but the scheme enables us to find homes for cats that need exceptional care and treatment and it also frees space at the Shelter so that we can take in more cats that need our help.

Kanga and Tiger.
These two elderly siblings were still in search of a Foster home after living at the Shelter for over a year.

We also have a team of Short-Term foster carers who look after mums with young litters, or orphan litters that need hand raising. Without their help, we would have to employ staff to work through the night, which would be a massive burden on our budget. Once kittens are old enough to be neutered, they are returned to the Shelter so that they can be found permanent homes.

There are times when we have relied heavily on our foster carers to help us in emergency situations. Never more so than in 2016, when we took in nine kittens that had been abandoned by a heartless person who left them in the rain with only an old chip box for cover.

In these conditions, the kittens would have died, had it not been for the kindness of a passer-by who found them, and contacted 'Friends of Ferals' who do a sterling job helping to control and monitor the feral population in and around Sheffield. Unfortunately, they were short of space, but after contacting us, we provided emergency care.

These three kittens were only four weeks old and too young to be without their mother, so one of our Foster carers immediately took them in until they were old enough to be adopted.

Jason, Laura and
Bradley in their
foster home

The older of the kittens were cared for by the Shelter staff.

As the kittens were found during the weekend that our 2016 Olympic team were returning home, they were all named to honour our sporting heroes. They had health problems to overcome, and needed a lot of TLC, but a few months after taking them in, they all found their forever homes.

Chapter 6 - Our Identity

"We are distinct because we are local and make every effort to socialise cats before adoption"

Our identity is important to us because as a local charity, we believe that we have a unique role to play in helping the people of Sheffield, as well as the local cat population. We are sympathetic and understanding to people who genuinely need our help when they are no longer able to care for their pets, and we prioritise and take in cats that are most at risk. We care for cats in a distinct way and often take in animals that other rescue centres are unable to. And we make every effort to socialise cats and match them to the right family when they are re-homed.

Our corporate logos and colours have changed over the years to reflect what we do.

Our fist logo, adopted in the 1960s, bears no relation to the message that we convey today, but is an interesting part of our history.

In 1997, our 100th year, a local company, 'Two Cats Too Support' designed and donated this logo to us. Known as the 'Fat Cat' it retained the corporate colours of yellow and blue. Although popular, the design eventually became problematic because it didn't differentiate the Shelter in a crowded market.

The Sheffield Cats Shelter

Because the public often assumed that we were part of a national charity, we rebranded in 2012 with this colourful logo, designed and donated by a Sheffield Hallam University student.

THE SHEFFIELD CATS SHELTER
Caring for cats and kittens since 1897

But, during our incorporation process, professional advisers recommended that we relaunch our new company with a fresh look. As this coincided with our 120-year anniversary, we are celebrating our milestone year with a new image that we hope will last for many years.

Rosie, *a beautiful kitten who came to the Shelter with her mother and siblings when she was only a week old*

Chapter 7 - Our people

*"Our staff couldn't run the charity without
the support of volunteers"*

The Sheffield Cats Shelter relies on a diverse range of people to manage and run the charity and who all play a vital part in caring for animals in need of help. These dedicated people include:

Director/Trustee

The Trustees of the Shelter became Directors in 2017 and along with our Company Secretary, they are ultimately responsible for the fiscal management of the charity, the employment of staff, fundraising, and policy decisions. This is a complex role and comes with responsibilities to the Charity Commission and Companies House. It's an unpaid position, that needs dedication and a variety of skills.

Staff

Our Charity Manager oversees the day-to-day running of the organisation and our staff have a wide range of skills and knowledge to draw on to deal with routine daily operations.

Experts in cat care, the Shelter staff are primarily responsible for the welfare of our animals. Our retail staff manage the shop which brings in finance to support the charity. All the people we employ do vital work for us but they couldn't do this without the support of volunteers.

Volunteers

We rely on a small army of volunteers who help run our charity, as well as taking part in our many fundraising activities. Volunteers carry out a range of duties including admin support, cat room duties, reception duties, general assistant, and even gardening, driving and small maintenance tasks.

Volunteers gain from their experience and in many cases, take the opportunity to learn skills that help them into employment. Volunteering is also a wonderful way to meet new people whilst making a positive contribution to society.

Volunteers in 1978, helping with the many cats that we have re-homed.

Harry, *a shy boy who was found as a stray. He spent time in a foster home with his siblings and soon came out of his shell.*

Chapter 8 - Funding

"Every penny helps"

Running costs

We rescue and rehome around 400 destitute cats and kittens each year, and it sometimes takes weeks of medical treatment and nursing care to get them into shape for re-homing. Our philosophy is to provide cats with whatever help they need, which means that our annual running costs, including veterinary fees, are exceptionally high.

But it doesn't take much to support us. And every penny helps.

- £1 can feed a cat for one day
- £5 will microchip a cat so that it will never be homeless again
- £10 will buy flea and worm treatment which is vital to cat health care
- £50 will neuter a cat which will stop more homeless kittens

As well as providing direct support to our cats, donations also help us to pay for:

Accommodation

- Regular costs include:
  - o lighting
  - o heating
  - o council tax
  - o phone bills
  - o maintenance costs
  - o insurance

Staff

- Who are dedicated to helping cats

Transport

- To maintain our van, we need to pay for:
  - o Petrol
  - o Insurance
  - o Road tax

Cat care and cleaning

- Keeping our shelter clean means buying:
  - o Cat litter
  - o Cat friendly cleaning products

Administration

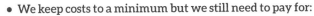
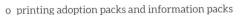

- We keep costs to a minimum but we still need to pay for:
  - o printing adoption packs and information packs
  - o a website and social media
  - o keeping in touch with members and volunteers

(Cartoons by curiouscatcreative.co.uk)

Raising Funds

"So, that's 7,093 cats, 988 dogs, 3 rabbits, 6 birds, a fox cub and a monkey"

Although the Barker family met initial set-up costs, fundraising has always been integral to the charity.

Early money raising efforts include a concert in 1902 which was reported in the local press:

Sheffield Daily Telegraph: Wednesday 12 March 1902
SHEFFIELD CATS SHELTER

Last night an excellent concert was given in the reception room at the Cutlers' Hall, in aid of the Cat's Shelter. Broomspring Lane, Sheffield. The entertainment was organised by Miss D. Davis, and there was a large audience. The institution was opened in January. 1897, for lost and starving pussies, and the number received during the past year reached 1,560. The object is not to provide a permanent home for cats but to reduce the number of homeless creatures wandering about, un-noticed, and un-cared for. The shelter is managed by a committee, and supported solely by voluntary contributions. The Patronesses are the Duchess of Portland and the Dowager Countess of Wharncliffe. The hon. Secretary is Miss D, Ibbotson, and the hon. treasurer Miss. J Barker. The following programme was gone through and the items much enjoyed, particularly the humorous songs of Mr W. Chatterton Adams: - violin solo, "Romance" (Elgar), Miss Nora Carter; song, "Who'll buy my lavender" (German), Mrs. John Cocker: song, "The old grey fox" (M Valerie White), Mr Arthur Davy; piano solo, "2nd Scherzo, Op. 31" (Chopin), Fraulein Lutze ; song, "Sweet and low" (Stephen Adams), Miss Gertrude Davis; song, "Paddy Murphy" (J. MacCallum), Mr W. Chatterton Adams; song, "Slave song" (Riego), Mrs. John Cocker: song, "Phil the Fluter" (W.P French), Mr W. Chatterton Adams: piano solo, "Frudlings rauschen" (Linding), Miss Carter; song, "My dreams" (Tosti), Mr Arthur Davy; violin solo, "Un soir a Poitici" (Guido Papini), Miss Nora Carter; song, "The Nights" (Murray), Miss Gertrude Davis; duologue, "A Pair of Lunatics," Miss Josephine Baines and Mr. H. Manby Colegrave.

The following year, this appeal appeared in the same paper under their 'Current Topics' heading:

Sheffield Daily Telegraph: Wednesday 25 February 1903

"The cats will mew, and the dog will have its day." And a very hard day it sometimes is. The fate of the dog, after all, is not quite so bad as that of the cat. The hearthrug pet is happy enough as long as it has a home assured, but those of us (writes "Rambler") whose calling takes them into the streets in the early hours of the morning know how many cats have no homes. At holiday seasons, it is distressing to be followed by the houseless ones who mew piteously after they have followed you closely, walking through the thoroughfares, and, by way of assuring you their friendship, stiffen their tails against your legs from time to time, to find that you shut the door upon them. Sheffield has a good dogs' home, which, it is pleasant to know, is in a position to do its work well. Perhaps it is not so well known that Sheffield has also a "cats shelter" into which last year were brought over 2,000 cats and kittens, many of them in a deplorable condition of starvation and disease. The committee who interest themselves in this humane work find themselves in debt, their regular income falling short of the necessary expenditure. The committee, therefore would like more annual subscribers. How many they have now I know not, but there must be other kind-hearted people who would give a small annual amount if they only knew the suffering the shelter prevents. The household cat is as useful as the household dog, and entitled to equal consideration. This is not the first time "Rambler" has appealed on behalf of the cats shelter, and he hopes that the result will revive interest in the merciful work now being done, largely at their own expense, by several worthy people.

Offering accommodation to a small number of cats as "boarders" brought in a small income.

1905, The Sheffield Red Book : Page 157
SHELTER FOR LOST AND STARVING CATS, 106, GELL STREET
(Entrance Broom Spring Lane)

The Sheffield Shelter for Lost and Starving Cats was first opened in January, 1897, and is doing an increasingly useful work, the number of cats and kittens received during the past year exceeding 2,200. The object of the shelter is not to provide a permanent home for cats, but to reduce the number of homeless creatures wandering about, unnoticed, uncared for, until they die of starvation or become victims of some form of cruelty. The majority of cats received have to be destroyed, owing to illness, accident and disease, and this is done in a merciful manner by means of chloroform. There is also accommodation for a limited number of cats as "boarders" at a moderate charge per week. The Shelter is managed by a committee and supported solely by voluntary contributions. Patronesses, Her Grace the Duchess of Portland, and the Dowager Countess of Wharncliffe; hon secretary, Mrs. Millward, 67 Wostenholm road; hon. Treasurer. Miss J Barker, the Rookery, Broomhall park.

The secretary of the Shelter in 1908, a Mr E Millward, tried to raise funds by sending this letter to the local press:

Sheffield Daily Telegraph: September 29th, 1908
EVERY CAT'S DAY

Sir, - as October 1st has been designated "Every Cat's Day" – on which date the public are requested to send the small sum of one shilling to the nearest Cats Home - I venture to draw the attention of your readers to the Sheffield Cats Shelter, 106 Gell Street.

This institution has been quietly doing an excellent work for the past 11 years.

Both from a humanitarian, and also a sanitary aspect, no one can dispute the need for such institutions in all large towns and cities, and it can only be because the public do not fully understand the nature of the work that there are not more subscribers.

Already this year, 2,260 lost and "not wanted" cats have been received in the Sheffield Shelter. The majority of these have, been mercifully destroyed, and thus delivered from a life which in innumerable cases was a burden owing to illness, accident or ill-usage. So far no grant had been received from the city authorities, although such a work - on sanitary grounds alone – it entitles to municipal support.

A report of the Sheffield Cats Shelter will gladly be sent on application to the hon secretary, 67, Wostenholm Road – Yours Truly – E MILLWARD

Jane Barker made a determined effort to get support from the local council during the first AGM in 1912. The views she expressed are understandably misguided, as she didn't have the knowledge and understating that we have today about cat behaviour, and the control of diseases. This heart-breaking summary of the meeting appeared in the local press.

Sheffield Daily Telegraph: Tuesday 14 May 1912

HOME-SICK CATS
WHY SHEFFIELD SHELTER "REFUSES" BOARDERS
CIVIC AID NEEDED

Lack of financial aid, largely due to insufficient public interest in the valuable and humane work of the Sheffield Shelter for Lost and Starving Cats, is making it increasingly difficult for the committee to adequately carry on their work. At the annual meeting, which was held at the Cutler's Hall, yesterday, under the presidency of Miss Barker, the opinion was reiterated that work was of such a necessitous character that it was deserving of the help of the civic authorities.

Miss Barker said that the time had come when they must, if it were at all possible, place the institution on a civic footing. Sheffield had the honor of being the second city in England – London being the first – to possess such a shelter, and seeing that the institution had proved its worth for 15 years, was it too much to expect that the city should come forward and assist the funds in order to obviate the closing of the Shelter in the future? Miss Barker said that she felt very hopeful that the Boy Scout movement would foster greater interest in the welfare of animals, especially among boys.

In their annual report, the committee intimated that as a result of past experience, they had finally decided to discontinue taking cats as boarders. "The cat," the report continues, "is a highly nervous animal and its health is seriously affected by home-sickness. The presence of other cats in the same position appears to have a depressing effect, and it is remarkable how soon a cat under these conditions may become ill. A journey, perhaps by train, or through crowded streets, the strange surroundings, coupled with the sudden loss of friends, may soon reduce a happy healthy cat to a heap of misery, and in spite of all one can do, sickness may set in and the cat be dead in little more than two days."

During the time the shelter had been in existence, 30,000 homeless and not-wanted animals had been received. The number of cats received during the past year amounted to 3,503. Of this number, 2,009 were lost cats, 1,413 sick or "not-wanteds," and 81 "deserteds" or animals left in empty houses. A large majority had to be destroyed each year, and this was done as painlessly as possible. It was most advisable that messengers sent with cats should be known to be thoroughly trustworthy, particularly when money was sent with the animals. Cases had been known when the cat sent had never arrived at the Shelter, and nothing further had been heard as to its fate.

The financial statement showed that receipts amounted to £134 18s 11d, and that there was a balance in hand of £4 1s 1d.

Miss Barker moved, and Mr. R Holmes seconded, the adoption of the report and financial statement, which was carried.

Mr. Arthur J. Coke, of London, secretary of Our Dumb Friends League, addressed the meeting on the many phases of the work of the League, particularly calling attention to the League's work with reference to lost and starving cats.

These early attempts to attract funding did however reach some people. An article in the Sheffield Independent on 21 July 1927 reported that a Miss Lydia Eliza Marriott of Nottingham, who had died on 29 April that year, left an estate worth £2,363. Other than the £10 that she left to each of her three executors and her personal effects to a Mr Edward Merton, the residue of her property, was willed on trust to the Shelter. This was a significant legacy.

The local press was used on a regular basis by Jane Barker, to raise interest in her work and attract support. This article, appeared under the "General Topic Column":

Sheffield Independent: Friday 29 November 1935

Miss Barker, the treasurer of the Cats Shelter in Gell Street, told me yesterday that cats become so attached to a home that in many cases they will not leave it when the tenants go, or if they do go they will return to the old home in a short time.

When they do return, however, they find their old place in ruins and all they can do is roam about the streets without food or without a drink. Their lot, said Miss Barker, is terrible.

Many of our early financial records are missing, but World War II clearly influenced the Shelter's fortunes. In 1941, a deficit was recorded for the first time. At £116 this was a huge amount and represented 17% of the £700 annual running costs. The Shelter's AGM minutes that year attribute the loss of income to:

- a drop in the number of boarders, and hence boarding fees
- more cats and dogs being admitted by people who feared losing their home (and never collecting them)
- the need to attract more 'subscribers'.

On top of this, for many weeks there was no gas supply so the lethal chambers were out of use.

This poetic extract from the minutes' is a lovely refection on a war-torn society:

In these sad times, great causes appeal for or help and human suffering must come first but even so the dogs and cats need not be denied the crumbs that fall from their masters' table.

The 1941 AGM minutes also list the number of animals that the Shelter received that year. Along with 7,093 cats and 988 dogs, a further 67 dogs were passed to the Dogs' Home, and the Shelter also took in 3 rabbits, 6 birds, a fox cub, and a monkey!

Telephones - - Gell Street—20656.   Attercliffe—42108.

Subscriptions and Donations Thankfully Received.

"They have no money with which to fight their cause: no Press to make known their miseries; no language in which to tell of their sufferings." Anon.

45th ANNUAL REPORT
of the

SHEFFIELD SHELTER
for

LOST and STARVING CATS

112 and 114 GELL STREET.   Open Daily up to 10 p.m.
Attercliffe Branch: 331 Attercliffe Common.

1941.

Patroness: HER GRACE THE DUCHESS OF PORTLAND.

Committee:

Miss G. ASHBERRY, 112 Westbourne Road, 10.
Miss BARKER, The Rookery, 27 Collegiate Crescent, 10.
Miss BRADLEY, 28 Mylnhurst Road.
Mrs. FINCH, 442 Glossop Road, 10.
Mrs. GIRDWOOD, Norfolk Lodge, Hollow Meadows, nr. Sheffield
Mrs. GREGORY ROSE-INNES, Leam, Grindleford.
Mrs. ARTHUR NEAL, Thurlstone.
Mrs. MACLAURIN, 106 Westbourne Road, 10.
Mrs. WATKINS, 1 Whirlow Park Road, 11.
Mrs. KELK, White House, Whirlow Lane, 11.
Mrs. CASSERE, 325 Millhouses Lane, 11.

Hon. Secretary: Miss ATKINS, 28 Mylnhurst Road.

Hon. Treas.: Miss J. BARKER, The Rookery, 27 Collegiate Crescent.

Caretakers: Gell Street—Mr. & Mrs. Barton. Attercliffe—Mrs. Hollis.

"Cruelty to cats shows a complete misunderstanding of one of the most sensitive animals in nature. . . . . It is vulgar stupidity."
Beverley Nichols.

Parker Bros., Vicar Lane, Sheffield.

RECEIPTS AND PAYMENTS ACCOUNT FOR THE YEAR ENDED 31st DECEMBER, 1941.

RECEIPTS.

	£ s d
To Balance at Bank 1st January 1941	38 3 11
Less Balance due to Treasurer	33 9 0
	4 14 3
Subscriptions and Donations	71 6 4
Received with and for Cats	59 13 10
Scrapping Dogs	30 9 6
Boarding Cats	47 19 8
Interest on Investments	43 2 0
Proceeds of Bring and Buy Sale	25 0 0
A Friend per Miss Atkins	50 0 0
Grant from City Council	— — —
Refund of Income Tax deducted from Interest on Investments	4 9 3
Sundries	1 1 4
Insurance Rebate	0 18 1
Balance due to Treasurer, 31st December, 1941	136 10 8
Less Balance at Bank do.	20 2 9
	116 7 11
	£700 16 4

PAYMENTS.

	£ s d
By Wages and National Insurance	268 4 5
Rent and Rates	42 17 0
Gas, Coal and Electricity	50 1 0
Milk, Meat, Fish, etc.	21 18 6
Petrol, Oil, etc.	48 15 0
Repairs to Motor Vans	63 11 6
Tax on Motor Vans	55 0 0
Garage of Motor Vans	24 3 0
Insurance (including Vans)	13 8 0
Telephone	17 17 4
Household Requisites and Repairs	21 0 0
Printing and Advertising	19 9 9
Window Cleaning, Sawdust etc.	3 6 3
Sundries	2 12 6
Auditing Accounts and Cheque Books	1 1 0
Bank Commission and Cheque Books	— — —
	£700 16 4

I have examined the above Receipts and Payments Account with the Books, Accounts and Vouchers produced and certify the same to be in accordance therewith.

W. G. HAWSON & CO.,
Chartered Accountants.

Hartshead Chambers, Sheffield 1,
16th April, 1942.

SHEFFIELD CATS' SHELTERS.

The year just past has been the most anxious since our first Shelter was opened in 1897. Our resources have been diminishing of late years and now the Treasurer has had for the first time to face a deficit—a serious one of £116. This disheartening state of affairs is entirely due to the war. Certain sources of income have failed and for the time being the boarding of cats has almost ceased; there are fewer owners going away and needing their cats to be cared for and the extreme difficulty of getting food has obliged us to refuse most applications. But the chief trouble has been the need for more subscribers—without larger funds the work cannot be carried on. Surely there are in Sheffield enough people interested in the cat population to give the much-needed support. In these sad times great causes appeal for our help and human suffering must come first but even so the dogs and the cats need not be denied the crumbs that fall from their masters' table.

The year 1941 opened gloomily—there were still starving cats wandering among the ruins of bombed houses and those had to be rescued wherever possible. Owners, fearing more raids, were bringing their cats and dogs to be destroyed while a large number of cats, at one time as many as 40 were being cared for at Gell Street till their homeless owners could get new houses. Many of these cats were never fetched away; many were never paid for. In addition to these worries there was for many weeks no gas supply and the lethal chambers could not be used at either Shelter. Then, to make matters still worse, Mr. Barton was very ill for some time. Altogether the first months of the year were a nightmare and but for the brave spirit of our caretakers at both Shelters and the help of our two R.S.P.C.A. Inspectors we could not have carried on.

Though things are generally much quieter than in the hectic days following the raids there is always plenty to be done. There are a good many street accidents when poor, mutilated cats have to be fetched and humanely destroyed as quickly as possible. There are not infrequent cases of cats, often families of kittens running wild in gardens and quite impossible to catch. No one troubles to inform the Shelter till matters are desperate. People are earnestly requested to report such cases at once whenever they know of them. Then too the cats are the saddest perhaps, the numberless host of "not wanted" cats. The work of our Shelters is sad work and we are greatly indebted to Mr. and Mrs. Barton at Gell Street and to Mr. and Mrs. Hollis at Attercliffe for the real interest they have taken in the cause of stray and suffering animals, not sparing themselves but doing their utmost to help wherever it has been needed.

The number of animals received at the two Shelters during the year are as follows:—

Cats (stray, ill and not wanted)	7093
Dogs (brought to be destroyed)	988
Stray Dogs (passed on to Dogs' Home)	67
Rabbits	3
Fox Cub	1
Monkey	1
Birds	6
	8159

SUBSCRIPTIONS AND DONATIONS.

	£ s d		£ s d
A Mother's Teaching	0 2 6	Mrs. Hibberd	0 5 0
Miss Armstrong	0 12 6	Miss Higton	0 5 0
Miss G. Ashberry	1 1 0	The Misses Hodgkinson, Retford	2 2 0
Miss Atkins	1 1 0	Mrs. Howe	0 2 6
Miss A. Atkins	0 5 0	Mrs. Kelk	0 10 0
Mrs. Bagshawe	0 1 0	Mrs. Kirkby	0 2 6
Mrs. E. Barber (the late)	0 2 6	Mrs. Laycock, Scarborough (don.)	3 3 0
Miss Barker	1 1 0	Mrs. R. Leader	0 10 0
Miss J. Barker	1 1 0	Mrs. Maclaurin	0 10 0
Miss Barratt	0 2 6	Miss H. MacGillevray	0 2 6
Miss Sybil Beal	0 5 0	Miss A. Marples	0 10 0
Mrs. Beardsley	0 5 0	Mrs. A. Marples	0 10 0
Mr. P. Bowker	0 5 0	Mrs. Maxfield	0 2 6
Miss Bradley	1 0 0	Miss Mitchell, Retford (don.)	1 0 0
Mrs. Bremner (2 years)	2 0 0	Miss E. Moxon	0 10 0
Miss W. A. Butler	2 2 0	Miss Naylor	0 10 0
Cats' Protection League	1 0 0	Mrs. Neal, Thurlstone	0 5 0
Miss D. Cole	1 1 0	Mrs. Oakley	1 0 0
Mrs. Cooley	0 2 6	Mrs. Outram, Rawmarsh	0 10 0
Dr. Coombe	0 6 8	Mrs. Parsonage (collected by)	0 4 6
Mrs. Coote	0 10 0	Mrs. Payne	1 10 0
Miss Coram	0 10 0	Mrs. Pryce	0 2 6
Mrs. Crabtree	0 10 0	Mr. Percy Reynolds	0 2 6
Mrs. Croft	0 8 0	Mrs. Richardson	0 5 0
Mr. Croft	0 5 0	Mrs. Riddle	0 5 0
Mr. W. A. Croft	0 2 6	Mrs. Rose-Innes	0 5 0
Mrs. Deakin	0 5 0	(don.)	0 15 0
Miss A. M. Deakin, Bamford	0 2 6	Mrs. Sellars	5 0 0
Miss Ellis	0 10 0	Miss Taylor (don.)	5 0 0
Miss Ellis (two friends)	0 2 6	Miss Thorp	0 2 6
Miss Favell	0 2 6	Mr. J. Walker	0 10 0
Mrs. Finch	1 1 0	Mrs. Walker (don.)	5 0 0
Miss Gillott	0 2 6	Mr. T. Ward	0 2 6
Miss J. Gillott	0 2 6	Mrs. J. C. Wood	0 2 6
Mr. F. Gillott	0 2 6	Mrs. E. Wigfall	0 10 0
Mrs. Girdwood	0 10 0	Mrs. Williamson, Dawlish	0 5 0
Mrs. Girdwood (donation)	3 0 0	Amounts under 2/6	0 5 0
Mrs. Graves	1 0 0	Collected in Shelter Boxes (Gell Street)	4 15 0
Mr. E. Barrett Hague	3 13 6	Collected in Shelter Boxes (Attercliffe)	2 4 8
Miss E. E. Barrett Hague (the late)	3 13 6		
Miss Hammond	0 5 0		
Miss Hancock	0 11 0		
Miss J. Herring	0 5 0		
Mrs. Hewitt	0 5 0		
Mr. W. H. Hewitt (2 years)	1 0 0	Total	£71 6 4

These early records confirm the constant challenge to raise funds to meet annual running costs, which rise annually as this summary of finances in the 1980/90s shows:

Year	Income £	Expenditure £
1983	5,000	5,400
1984	7,800	8,100
1985	14,500	13,400
1986	12,800	13,700
1987	21,700	18,700
1988	24,000	23,400
1989	26,155	26,630
1990	26,354	25,084
1991	38,442	30,935
1992	81,858	38,442

Over the years, the Shelter has received some regular sources of income including:

Boarding fees

Although they didn't contribute a great deal, boarding fees provided income until January 1994. As late as 1987 we only charged £1.25 per day and they remained as low as £1.50 in 1993, the year before boarding ceased.

Adoption Fees

Adoption fees are an important revenue, but they are significantly lower than the costs we incur to rehome a cat. In 1994, they were set at £21, which was a fraction of the £120 that it cost at that time to re-home a cat. Fees were increased in 1998, but remained low at £30 for adults and £40 for kittens. 2003 saw another modest increase to £45 for adults and £55 for kittens. Fees are kept low to make adopting accessible, but we hope that the public will understand the need to review our prices annually, and if they are able to, make a donation to help meet the cost of readying each cat for a new home.

Membership fees

The earliest recorded membership fees are in 1986, when annual subscriptions were increased to £5, but pensioners and the unemployed paid £1. In 1996, we introduced life membership at £150.

We now have a robust list of members who support us with subscriptions and by attending our fundraising events. But we always welcome new members!

Volunteer help

Volunteers save us enormous amounts of money that we would otherwise have to spend on staff costs. They have helped the charity from the very beginning, but since the 1970/80s we have relied on them to help with duties other than direct cat care. For example, in 1986 we took on two 'community' part time workers who helped to improve the efficiency of the Shelter.

Direct Fundraising

The regular income we receive is vital to us, but not sufficient to meet the cost of running the Shelter. We are therefore dependent on fundraising and legacies. Some of the most successful fundraising activities have included:

1985

- A publicity day in Fargate
- A stall at the cat show at the Doncaster Race Course
- An enterprising volunteer spent a lot of time making and selling home-made jams, marmalades, pickles and cakes
- A Christmas food appeal brought in 2,700 tins of cat food

1986

- A crisis appeal was issued for new Committee Members to help fundraise.

1987

- £1,000 was raised by holding two fayres, and a further £250 at our Open Day.
- An idea was floated to hold "Junior" Committee Meetings to reach out to younger supporters.

1988

- A fundraising appeal was launched to purchase sign-posts from the main road to the Shelter.

1989

- A Flag day raised £450 which was attributed to collectors wearing 'publicity bibs'.

1990

- A photographic contest was held.
- A publicity stall raised £2,400, which by today's standards is outstanding.
- We had commercial sponsorship from 20 local firms plus donations of food from Pedigree.

1992

- A request to Crystal Peals Shopping Mall, for a share of the donations in their 'coin in a fountain'.
- We sold a selection of branded goods including Christmas cards, window stickers and pens.

1993

- A sponsored swim at Ponds Forge, followed by a float in the Lord Mayor's Parade. We won first prize for the most original float.
- A Christmas Fayre at the Sheffield Cathedral.

1994

- An Open Day, where we sold cat food at 20p a tin; provided face painting and held a picture competition from local nurseries. The Feline Theatre Company also put on a play to entertain our visitors.

1996

- 'Sponsor a cage' was an initiative to raise monies to help pay for the major refurbishments in 1996/7.

1998

- A legacy of £100,000 saved the Shelter from closing and the Trustees declared that it would 'secure the Shelter for many years to come.'

1999

- A gazebo was purchased so that we could set up a stall at local fairs.

2011

- Our first summer Fun Run was organised by our Cat Care Manager. This has now become an annual event and supports our Foster scheme.

Today we rely on open days and street collections to raise funds, along with auctions, raffles and attending local fairs and markets. We also have supporters who raise sponsorship by taking part in events such as the Sheffield marathon and the Three Peaks Challenge. And our volunteers have come up with some inventive fundraising efforts, including a fire walk, and a Rock Music event (Mogstock) which we hope will become a regular event.

Donny, *who was left living outside after his owner sadly passed away.*

꧁ Our retail outlet ꧂

We sell donated goods to raise funds and to capitalise on the generosity of our supporters, we opened our first retail outlet in 2014 at 285 Ecclesall Road. All items are checked for cleanliness and condition and a small range of new and branded goods are also available.

285 Ecclesall Road.

Substandard items are also welcome because we operate a recycling programme that brings in additional funding.

In 2014, Jack, a black and white Tom, who lived with his family in Gleadless decided to go for a walk and got lost. After walking miles, he found himself on Ecclesall Road, and noticed the Shelter's charity shop and decided to wander in. Perhaps to ask for directions? He quickly made friends with the staff, who took him to the vets to check for a microchip. Although he had one, it did not yield sufficient information, so we put him up at the Shelter and posted his details on Facebook. His family soon contacted us and he was reunited with his owners.

Corporate Support

We also receive support from several businesses who donate cat food, beds, scratch posts and toys to us, or enter partnership agreements that help us to raise funds. We have also been fortunate to receive grants to help with specific projects. In particular, 'Support Adoption for Pets' has helped us to improve our heating system and to purchase a much-needed new van in 2015.

Dougal, *a charming boy who was quickly re-homed by the Shelter*

Please see
Chapter 9 for
ways that
you can help.

Chapter 9
Your Support Is Vital

"Your kindness can help"

Your kindness can help cats such as **Flash** who at 8 months old, was brought to the Shelter in 2013. He had a condition causing a dislocation of his back-knee caps which could only be corrected by surgery. His operation cost £1,000 but the kindness and generosity of the Sheffield public helped us to pay his veterinary fees.

Individuals

If you care about cats and would like to support the Shelter, please help us by:

- Becoming a member
- Donating
- Becoming a volunteer
- Fundraising for us
- Leaving a legacy

Businesses

If you are self-employed, or manage a company, you can support us whilst gaining benefits for your business. Organisations can achieve enhanced brand value by developing a positive relationship with our Charity, because your support will be recognised and helps to build trust and brand warmth because of your engagement with us, as a well-established organisation. Supporting the Sheffield Cats Shelter also fulfils Corporate Social Responsibility objectives, and not only brings a positive impact on your organisation, but can also provide an entire range of added value opportunities.

Please visit our website at **www.thesheffieldcatsshelter.org** for further details about the many ways that you can help our charity.

Thank you for your support

By engaging with our charity, you will get the satisfaction of knowing that your help will make a massive difference to all the stray and neglected cats and kittens we support and care for, as well as helping us to provide essential education and support on cat welfare. It also acknowledges the huge contribution that our staff and committed volunteer workforce makes.

The Sheffield Cats Shelter

1 Travis Place

Broomhall

Sheffield

S10 2BD

0114 272 4441

Registered Charity: 1172162

www.thesheffieldcatsshelter.org

Text CATS18 followed by the amount and send it to **70070**

APPENDIX 1

References

GRIFFIN, John D. 2001. The Don Pottery 1801-1893.

RSPCA. The Legacy of Benjamin Cartledge.
https://rspcasheffield.homeip.net/cgi-bin/displaypage.py?pageid=56

APPENDIX 2

Entries from the SHEFFIELD AND ROTHERHAM RED BOOK and Other Directories.

Sheffield and Rotherham Red Book : 1901 to 1923.
Sheffield City Archives.

The Sheffield and Rotherham Red Book and Almanac was an annual publication that listed all the official organisations of Sheffield and Rotherham for that year, including charities, societies, council departments, institutions etc. Copies of the Red Book are available at the Sheffield Library and Archives, from the late 1800s to 1924.

The earliest entry for our charity in the Red Book is in 1901. These extracts are reproduced as how they appear in the Sheffield Red Book.

1901

The Sheffield Red Book : Page 49

SHELTER FOR LOST AND STARVING CATS, 27, BROOMSPRING LANE.

The Sheffield Shelter for Lost and Starving Cats was first opened in January, 1897, and is doing an increasingly useful work, the number of cats and kittens received during the present year exceeding 1,200. The object of the shelter is not to provide a permanent home for cats, but to reduce the number of homeless creatures wandering about, unnoticed, uncared for, until they die of starvation or become victims of some form of cruelty. The majority of cats received have to be destroyed, owing to illness, accident and disease, and this is done in a merciful manner by means of chloroform. The Shelter is managed by a committee and supported solely by voluntary contributions. Patronesses, Her Grace the Duchess of Portland, and the Dowager Countess of Wharncliffe; hon secretary, Miss D Ibbottson; hon. Treasurer. Miss J Barker, the Rookery, Broomhall park; hon. Veterinary surgeon, Mr. Tom C. Fletcher, M.R.C.V.S. 3 Ellin-street, Moor.

1902

The Sheffield Red Book : Page 53

SHELTER FOR LOST AND STARVING CATS, 27, BROOMSPRING LANE.

The Sheffield Shelter for Lost and Starving Cats was first opened in January, 1897, and is doing an increasingly useful work, the number of cats and kittens received during the present year amounting to 1,600. The object of the shelter is not to provide a permanent home for cats, but to reduce the number of homeless creatures wandering about, unnoticed, uncared for, until they die of starvation or become victims of some form of cruelty. The majority of cats received have to be destroyed, owing to illness, accident and disease, and this is done in a merciful manner by means of chloroform. The Shelter is managed by a committee and supported solely by voluntary contributions. Patronesses, Her Grace the Duchess of Portland, and the Dowager Countess of Wharncliffe; hon secretary, Miss D Ibbotson; hon. Treasurer. Miss J Barker, the Rookery, Broomhall park; hon. Veterinary surgeon, Mr. Tom C. Fletcher, M.R.C.V.S. 3 Ellin-street, Moor.

1903

The Sheffield Red Book : Page 55

SHELTER FOR LOST AND STARVING CATS, 27, BROOMSPRING LANE.

The Sheffield Shelter for Lost and Starving Cats was first opened in January, 1897, and is doing an increasingly useful work, the number of cats and kittens received during the present year amounting to 1,950. The object of the shelter is not to provide a permanent home for cats, but to reduce the number of homeless creatures wandering about, unnoticed, uncared for, until they die of starvation or become victims of some form of cruelty. The majority of cats received have to be destroyed, owing to illness, accident and disease, and this is done in a merciful manner by means of chloroform. The Shelter is managed by a committee and supported solely by voluntary contributions. Patronesses, Her Grace the Duchess of Portland, and the Dowager Countess of Wharncliffe; hon secretary, Miss D Ibbotson; hon. Treasurer. Miss J Barker, the Rookery, Broomhall park; hon. Veterinary surgeon, Mr. Tom C. Fletcher, M.R.C.V.S. 3 Ellin-street, Moor.

1904

The Sheffield Red Book : Page 60

SHELTER FOR LOST AND STARVING CATS, 27, BROOMSPRING LANE.

The Sheffield Shelter for Lost and Starving Cats was first opened in January, 1897, and is doing an increasingly useful work, the number of cats and kittens received during the past year exceeding 2,000. The object of the shelter is not to provide a permanent home for cats, but to reduce the number of homeless creatures wandering about, unnoticed, uncared for, until they die of starvation or become victims of some form of cruelty. The majority of cats received have to be destroyed, owing to illness, accident and disease, and this is done in a merciful manner by means of chloroform. The Shelter is managed by a committee and supported solely by voluntary contributions. Patronesses, Her Grace the Duchess of Portland, and the Dowager Countess of Wharncliffe; hon secretary, Mrs. Millward, 67 Wostenholm road; hon. Treasurer. Miss J Barker, the Rookery, Broomhall park; hon. veterinary surgeon, Mr. Tom C. Fletcher, M.R.C.V.S. 3 Ellin-street, Moor.

1905

The Sheffield Red Book : Page 157

SHELTER FOR LOST AND STARVING CATS, 27, BROOMSPRING LANE.

The Sheffield Shelter for Lost and Starving Cats was first opened in January, 1897, and is doing an increasingly useful work, the number of cats and kittens received during the past year exceeding 2,200. The object of the shelter is not to provide a permanent home for cats, but to reduce the number of homeless creatures wandering about, unnoticed, uncared for, until they die of starvation or become victims of some form of cruelty. The majority of cats received have to be destroyed, owing to illness, accident and disease, and this is done in a merciful manner by means of chloroform. There is also accommodation for a limited number of cats as "boarders" at a moderate charge per week. The Shelter is managed by a committee and supported by voluntary contributions. Patronesses, Her Grace the Duchess of Portland, and the Dowager Countess of Wharncliffe; hon secretary, Mrs. Millward, 67 Wostenholm road; hon. Treasurer. Miss J Barker, the Rookery, Broomhall park.

1906

The Sheffield Red Book : Page 190

SHELTER FOR LOST AND STARVING CATS

106, GELL STREET (Entrance Broom Spring Lane)

The Sheffield Shelter for Lost and Starving Cats was first opened in January, 1897, and is doing an increasingly useful work, the number of cats and kittens received during the past year exceeding 2,300. The object of the shelter is not to provide a permanent home for cats, but to reduce the number of homeless creatures wandering about, unnoticed, uncared for, until they die of starvation or become victims of some form of cruelty. The majority of cats received have to be destroyed, owing to illness, accident and disease, and this is done in a merciful manner by means of chloroform. There is also accommodation for a limited number of cats as "boarders" at a moderate charge per week. The Shelter is managed by a committee and supported by voluntary contributions. Patronesses, Her Grace the Duchess of Portland, and the Dowager Countess of Wharncliffe; hon secretary, Mrs. Millward, 67 Wostenholm road; hon. Treasurer. Miss J Barker, the Rookery, Broomhall park; hon. veterinary surgeon, Mr. Jos, Abson, 58 Norfolk-street

1907

The Sheffield Red Book : Page 200

SHELTER FOR LOST AND STARVING CATS

106, GELL STREET (Entrance Broom Spring Lane)

The Sheffield Shelter for Lost and Starving Cats was first opened in January, 1897, and is doing an increasingly useful work, the number of cats and kittens received during the past year exceeding 2,500. The object of the shelter is not to provide a permanent home for cats, but to reduce the number of homeless creatures wandering about, unnoticed, uncared for, until they die of starvation or become victims of some form of cruelty. The majority of cats received have to be destroyed, owing to illness, accident and disease, and this is done in a merciful manner by means of chloroform. There is also accommodation for a limited number of cats as "boarders" at a moderate charge per week. The Shelter is managed by a committee and supported by voluntary contributions. Hon secretary, Mrs. Millward, 67 Wostenholm road; hon. Treasurer. Miss J Barker, the Rookery, Broomhall park; hon. veterinary surgeon, Mr. Jos, Abson, 53 Norfolk-street.

1908

The Sheffield Red Book : Page 222

SHELTER FOR LOST AND STARVING CATS

106, GELL STREET (Entrance Broom Spring Lane)

The Sheffield Shelter for Lost and Starving Cats was first opened in January, 1897, and is doing an increasingly useful work, the number of cats and kittens received during the past year exceeding 2,600. The object of the shelter is not to provide a permanent home for cats, but to reduce the number of homeless creatures wandering about, unnoticed, uncared for, until they die of starvation or become victims of some form of cruelty. The majority of cats received have to be destroyed, owing to illness, accident and disease, and this is done in a merciful manner by means of chloroform. There is also accommodation for a limited number of cats as "boarders" at a moderate charge per week. The Shelter is managed by a committee and supported by voluntary contributions. Hon secretary, Mrs. Millward, 67 Wostenholm road; hon. Treasurer. Miss J Barker, the Rookery, Broomhall park; hon. veterinary surgeon, Mr. Jos, Abson, 53 Norfolk-street.

1909

The Sheffield Red Book : Page 215

SHELTER FOR LOST AND STARVING CATS

106, GELL STREET (Entrance Broom Spring Lane)

The object of the shelter is not to provide a permanent home for cats, but to reduce the number of homeless creatures wandering about, unnoticed, uncared for, until they die of starvation or become victims of some form of cruelty. The majority of cats received have to be destroyed, owing to illness, accident and disease, and this is done in a merciful manner by means of chloroform. There is also accommodation for a limited number of cats as "boarders" at a moderate charge per week. The Shelter is managed by a committee and supported by voluntary contributions. Hon secretary, Mrs. Millward, 67 Wostenholm road; hon. Treasurer. Miss J Barker, the Rookery, Broomhall park; hon. veterinary surgeon, Mr. Jos, Abson, 53 Norfolk-street.

1910

The Sheffield Red Book : Page 203

SHELTER FOR LOST AND STARVING CATS

106, GELL STREET (Entrance Broom Spring Lane)

Is doing increasingly useful work, the number of cats and kittens received during the past year exceeding 3,200. The object of the shelter is not to provide a permanent home for cats, but to reduce the number of homeless creatures wandering about, unnoticed, uncared for, until they die of starvation or become victims of some form of cruelty. The majority of cats received have to be destroyed, owing to illness, accident and disease, and this is done in a merciful manner by means of chloroform. There is also accommodation for a limited number of cats as "boarders" at a moderate charge per week. The Shelter is managed by a committee and supported by voluntary contributions. Hon secretary, Mrs. Millward, 67 Wostenholm road; hon. Treasurer. Miss J Barker, the Rookery, Broomhall park; hon. veterinary surgeon, Mr. Jos, Abson, 53 Norfolk-street

1911

The Sheffield Red Book : Page 205

SHELTER FOR LOST AND STARVING CATS

106, GELL STREET (Entrance Broom Spring Lane)

Is doing increasingly useful work, the number of cats and kittens received during the past year exceeding 3,600. The object of the shelter is not to provide a permanent home for cats, but to reduce the number of homeless creatures wandering about, unnoticed, uncared for, until they die of starvation or become victims of some form of cruelty. The majority of cats received have to be destroyed, owing to illness, accident and disease, and this is done in a merciful manner by means of chloroform. There is also accommodation for a limited number of cats as "boarders" at a moderate charge per week. The Shelter is managed by a committee and supported by voluntary contributions. Hon secretary, Mrs. Millward, 67 Wostenholm road; hon. Treasurer. Miss J Barker, the Rookery, Broomhall park; hon. veterinary surgeon, Mr. Jos, Abson, 53 Norfolk-street

1912

The Sheffield Red Book : Page 218

SHELTER FOR LOST AND STARVING CATS

106, GELL STREET (Entrance Broom Spring Lane)

Is doing increasingly useful work, the number of cats and kittens received during the past year exceeding 3,700. The object of the shelter is not to provide a permanent home for cats, for to reduce the number of homeless creatures wandering about, unnoticed, uncared for, until they die of starvation or become victims of some form of cruelty. The majority of cats received have to be destroyed, owing to illness, accident and disease, and this is done in a merciful manner by means of chloroform. There is also accommodation for a limited number of cats and dogs as "boarders" at a moderate charge per week. The Shelter is managed by a committee and supported by voluntary contributions. Hon secretary, Mrs. Millward, 67 Wostenholm road; hon. Treasurer. Miss J Barker, the Rookery, Broomhall park; hon. veterinary surgeon, Mr. Jos, Abson, 53 Norfolk-street.

1913

The Sheffield Red Book : Page 237

SHELTER FOR LOST AND STARVING CATS

106, GELL STREET (Entrance Broom Spring Lane)

Is doing increasingly useful work, the number of cats and kittens received during the past year exceeding 4,000. The object of the shelter is not to provide a permanent home for cats, for to reduce the number of homeless creatures wandering about, unnoticed, uncared for, until they die of starvation or become victims of some form of cruelty. The majority of cats received have to be destroyed, owing to illness, accident and disease, and this is done in a merciful manner by means of chloroform. There is also accommodation for a limited number of cats and small dogs as "boarders" at a moderate charge per week. Lethal chambers for the merciful destruction of dogs are now kept on the premises. The Shelter is managed by a committee and supported by voluntary contributions. Hon secretary, Mrs. Millward, 67 Wostenholm road; hon. Treasurer. Miss J Barker, the Rookery, Broomhall park; hon. veterinary surgeon, Mr. Jos, Abson, 53 Norfolk-street.

1914

The Sheffield Red Book : Page 226

SHELTER FOR LOST AND STARVING CATS

106, GELL STREET (Entrance Broom Spring Lane)

Is doing increasingly useful work, nearly 4,000 cats having been received during the past year. The object of the shelter is not to provide a permanent home for cats, for to reduce the number of homeless creatures wandering about, unnoticed, uncared for, until they die of starvation or become victims of some form of cruelty. The majority of cats received have to be destroyed, owing to illness, accident and disease, and this is done in a merciful manner by means of chloroform. There is also accommodation for a limited number of cats and small dogs as "boarders" at a moderate charge per week. Lethal chambers for the merciful destruction of dogs are now kept on the premises. The Shelter is managed by a committee and supported by voluntary contributions. Hon secretary, Mrs. Millward, 67 Wostenholm road; hon. Treasurer. Miss J Barker, the Rookery, Broomhall park; hon. veterinary surgeon, Mr. Jos, Abson, 53 Norfolk-street.

1915

The Sheffield Red Book : Page 223

SHELTER FOR LOST AND STARVING CATS

106, GELL STREET (Entrance Broom Spring Lane)

There is accommodation for a limited number of cats and small dogs as "boarders" at a moderate charge per week. Lethal chambers for the merciful destruction of dogs are now kept on the premises. The Shelter is managed by a committee and supported by voluntary contributions. Hon secretary, Mrs. Millward, 67 Wostenholm road; hon. Treasurer. Miss J Barker, the Rookery, Broomhall park; hon. veterinary surgeon, Mr. Jos, Abson, 53 Norfolk-street.

1917

The Sheffield Red Book : Page 223

SHELTER FOR LOST AND STARVING CATS

106, GELL STREET (Entrance Broom Spring Lane)

An institution for the reception of all lost and not wanted cats. Number of cats received last year, over 3,000. Lethal chambers for the merciful destruction of both dogs and cats. A limited number of cats and small dogs received as boarders. Mainly supported by voluntary contributions. Hon secretary, Mrs. Millward, 67 Wostenholm road; hon. Treasurer. Miss J Barker, 27, Collegiate-crescent,

1918

The Sheffield Red Book : Page 223

SHELTER FOR LOST AND STARVING CATS

106, GELL STREET (Entrance Broom Spring Lane)

An institution for the reception of all lost and not wanted cats. Number of cats received last year, over 3,000. Lethal chambers for the merciful destruction of both dogs and cats. A limited number of cats and small dogs received as boarders. Mainly supported by voluntary contributions. Hon secretary, Mrs. Millward, 67 Wostenholm road; hon. Treasurer. Miss J Barker, 27, Collegiate-crescent,

1919

The Sheffield Red Book : Page 226

SHELTER FOR LOST AND STARVING CATS

106, GELL STREET (Entrance Broom Spring Lane)

An institution for the reception of all lost and not wanted cats. Number of cats received last year, 3,800. Lethal chambers for the merciful destruction of both dogs and cats. A limited number of cats and small dogs received as boarders. Mainly supported by voluntary contributions. Hon secretary, Mrs. Millward, 67 Wostenholm road; hon. Treasurer. Miss J Barker, 27, Collegiate-crescent,

1920

The Sheffield Red Book : Page 236

SHELTER FOR LOST AND STARVING CATS

106, GELL STREET (Entrance Broom Spring Lane)

An institution for the reception of all lost and not wanted cats. Number of cats received last year, 1,000. Lethal chambers for the merciful destruction of both dogs and cats. A limited number of cats and small dogs received as boarders. Mainly supported by voluntary contributions. Hon secretary, Mrs. Millward, 67 Wostenholm road; hon. Treasurer. Miss J Barker, 27, Collegiate-crescent,

1921

The Sheffield Red Book : Page 237

SHELTER FOR LOST AND STARVING CATS

106, GELL STREET (Entrance Broom Spring Lane)

An institution for the reception of all lost and not wanted cats. Number of cats received last year, 3,600. Lethal chambers for the merciful destruction of both dogs and cats. A limited number of cats and small dogs received as boarders. Mainly supported by voluntary contributions. Hon secretary, Mrs. Millward, 67 Wostenholm road; hon. Treasurer. Miss J Barker, 27, Collegiate-crescent,

1923

The Sheffield Red Book : Page 251

SHELTER FOR LOST AND STARVING CATS

106, GELL STREET (Entrance Broom Spring Lane)

An institution for the reception of all lost and not wanted cats. Number of cats received last year, 5,580. Lethal chambers for the merciful destruction of both dogs and cats. A limited number of cats and small dogs received as boarders. Mainly supported by voluntary contributions. Hon secretary, Mrs. Millward, 1 Ventnor-place; hon. Treasurer. Miss J Barker, 27, Collegiate-crescent,

·1924

The Sheffield Red Book : Page 251

SHELTER FOR LOST AND STARVING CATS

106, GELL STREET (Entrance Broom Spring Lane)

Telephone : Central 636

An institution for the reception of all lost and not wanted cats. Number of cats received last year, over 5,000. Lethal chambers for the merciful destruction of both dogs and cats. A limited number of cats and dogs received as boarders. Mainly supported by voluntary contributions. Hon secretary, Mrs.Hulme,3 Clarkson street; hon. Treasurer. Miss J Barker, 27, Collegiate-crescent,

Other Directories of Sheffield

White's Directory

The 1905 edition of White's Directory has the following entry:

Directory of Sheffield

1905

Sheffield Shelter for Lost and Starving Cats (Miss Sarah Dryhurst, Caretaker). 106 Gell Street.

This entry remains the same each year until 1930, except that mention of the caretaker is taken out.

Kelly's Directory

From 1931 to 1964, Kelly's Directory lists the shelter at 112 & 114 Gell Street. Between 1937 and 1942, a separate entry for the shelter appears:

1937

Kelly's Directory:

Court 7, 331 Attercliffe Common, Sheffield Shelter for Lost and Starving Cats

---

The Attercliffe Common premises are also mentioned in the main entry for the shelter:

1937

Kelly's Directory: page lxxxiv

Cats' Shelter, 112 & 114 Gell Street. First opened in 1897. The branch at 331 Attercliffe Common was opened in 1936. Open daily, up to 10 pm. The shelter is a temporary refuge, where cats are provided with food and warmth until claimed, sold or destroyed. Provision is also made for boarding cats; dogs as well as cats are humanely destroyed. Miss Edith Atkins, 28 Mylnhurst road, Ecclesall, hon secretary; Miss J Barker, 27 Collegiate crescent, hon, treasurer.

1942 page 276

Cats' Shelter, 112 & 114 Gell Street. First opened in 1897. The branch at 331 Attercliffe Common was opened in 1936. Open daily, up to 10 pm. The shelter is a temporary refuge, where cats are provided with food and warmth until claimed, sold or destroyed. Provision is also made for boarding cats; dogs as well as cats are humanely destroyed. Miss Edith Atkins, 28 Mylnhurst road, Ecclesall, hon secretary; Miss J Barker, 27 Collegiate crescent, hon, treasurer.

In 1965, the shelter is first listed at 1 Travis Place. However, the resident at 1 Travis Place is listed as Thomas Westran until 1968. In 1970 and 1971, Samuel Palmer is listed as the occupier until finally The Sheffield Cats Shelter is registered at 1 Travis Place in 1972.

The Sheffield and Telegraph Year Book

The Sheffield and Telegraph Year Book provides another source of information about the shelter.

Sheffield and Telegraph Year Book

1954. Page 159

Cats' Shelter, 112 & 114 Gell Street.

For the reception of lost and unwanted cats. Stay cats fetched free of charge. Dogs and cats humanely destroyed. Open daily from 9am to 10pm. Sundays included. (Tel 24441)

This entry remains the same but between 1958 and 1963 a shorted version appears.

The Sheffield and Telegraph Year Book

1958. Page 129

Cats' Shelter, 112 and 114 Gell Street.

Open daily 9am to 10pm, Sundays included. (Tel 24441)

The 1964/5 edition indicates that the shelter is open around the clock:

> ## The Sheffield and Telegraph Year Book
> ### 1964/65. Page 129
> ### Cats' Shelter, 112 and 114 Gell Street.
>
> Open all day and night, Sundays included. (Tel 24441)

Our entry the following year reflects our move to Travis Place:

> ## The Sheffield and Telegraph Year Book
> ### 1965/66. Page 129
> ### Cats' Shelter, 1 Travis Place (off Clarke Street) 10
>
> Late Gell Street. Open daily 9am to 10pm. (Tel 24441)
>
> hon. Secretary, Miss J Julien, 1 Collegiate Crescent, 10. hon. Treasurer A Thorpe, 785 Chesterfield Road, 8.